Wayne's College of Beauty

Wayne's College

T0154998

Wayne's College of Beauty

David Swanger

Winner of the John Ciardi Prize for Poetry
Selected by Colleen J. McElroy

 BkMk Press
University of Missouri-Kansas City

BkMk Press
University of Missouri-Kansas City
5101 Rockhill Road
Kansas city, Missouri 64110
(816) 235-2558 (voice)
(816) 235-2611 (fax)

Cover art: "Denied Reflection" by Antonia Riera
Author photo: Mark Gottlieb
Cover and interior book design: Susan L. Schurman
Associate Editor: Michelle Boisseau
Managing Editor: Ben Furnish
Printing: Walsworth Publishing Co., Marceline, Missouri

BkMk wishes to thank Bill Beeson, Kayleigh Butcher, Teresa Collins, Christopher Glenn, Kevin Kinghorn, Matthew Merryman, Andrés Rodríguez

The John Ciardi Prize for Poetry wishes to thank Lindsey Martin Bowen, Susan Cobin, Greg Field, Steve Gehrke, Jeannie Irons, Elaine K. Lally, Michael Nelson, Maryfrances Wagner

Previous winners of the John Ciardi Prize for Poetry: *The Portable Famine* by Rane Arroyo, selected by Robin Becker; *Fence Line* by Curtis Bauer, selected by Christopher Buckley; *Escape Artist* by Terry Blackhawk, selected by Molly Peacock; *Kentucky Swami* by Tim Skeen, selected by Michael Burns; *The Resurrection Machine* by Steve Gehrke, selected by Miller Williams

Library of Congress Cataloging-in-Publication Data

Swanger, David.
      Wayne's College of Beauty / David Swanger.
            p. cm.
Summary: "Divided into four thematic sections: Fathers and mothers/ husbands and wives, Water/war, Known/unknown, and Departure/arrival. Each section's poems explore its theme from perspectives that range from personal to the philosophical and metaphysical. These poems show beauty as a fundamental form of human understanding"—Provided by publisher.

      ISBN 1-886157-57-X (pbk. : alk. paper)
      I. Title.
      PS3569.W254W39 2006
      811'. 54--dc22   2006028198

W*ayne's College of Beauty* evokes neighborhoods and well-traveled paths. I was much impressed by the way music and metaphor fueled the narrative thread. The poet's strong sense of voice climbs above the resin of form. The cadence evokes imagery without losing the balance of sentiment and sentimentality. These poems are both hard-edged and beautiful, an exciting collection.

—Colleen J. McElroy
Final Judge
John Ciardi Prize for Poetry

Acknowledgements

Thanks, as always, to Lynn, the initial reader of everything. I am grateful to Steven Corey, Steven Kirschenbaum, Joe Stroud, and Gary Young, who read an early version of the manuscript; and to colleagues Charles Atkinson, Dion Farquhar, Doug McClellan, Priscilla Shaw, Robert Sward and Joan Zimmerman who offer smart suggestions on how to make a poem better.

These poems previously appeared in journals:

Poetry Northwest: "Wayne's College of Beauty," "Oedipus Irvington" and "Death School"
Sifrut: "Patriarch at the Lake"
Loophole: "Practice: Father and Son"
The Nebraska Review: "Debbie Does Daddy," (originally titled "Some Angel")
The Chariton Review: "The Past" and "White Out"
The Kansas Quarterly: "The Lessons" and "Asteroids Advance Toward Earth"
Quarry: "My Daughter's Morning"
Poetry Flash: "Natural Disaster," (originally titled "Ode")
The Georgia Review: "Cuckoo: Tuscany," "Gozo Poderoso," "Longer," "Languages I Don't Speak," "Scar," "Sloth," "Style," and "What the Wing Says"
America (Foley Award Winner): "Oxford,"

These poems are also anthologized:

The Geography of Home: California's Poetry of Place: "Wayne's College of Beauty,"
The Geography of Home: California's Poetry of Place and *Fresh Water: Poems from the Rivers, Lakes and Streams*: "Natural Disaster,"
Spreading the Word: Editors on Poetry and *Keener Sounds: Selected Poems from The Georgia Review*: "What the Wing Says"

For Lynn

Wayne's College of Beauty

13   Wayne's College of Beauty

I. Fathers and Mothers / Husbands and Wives

17   Patriarch at the Lake

18   Practice: Father and Son

19   Secrets

20   Assisted Living

22   Debbie Does Daddy

23   Oedipus Irvington

24   My Mother's Nudes

25   My Father: A Fiction

27   The Past

28   The Old Are Different

29   The Lessons

30   Alone

31   My Daughter's Morning

32   To Speak of the Woe

33   Sleeping with You

II. Water / War

37   Natural Disaster

38   Flood

39   Spoken Wading In

40   What Burns on Water

42   Seasons/Water

43   Jews, Those

44   The Coming War

45   Oh Dear Ones: 9/11/01

46   State of the Union: Feb. '03

47   Taking a Bite

48   Regime Change

49   The Uses of Sky

50   Whoever's Nearest

III. Known / Unknown

53   Asteroids Advance Toward Earth

54   Style

55   Aubade

56   Uncertainty Principle

57   Miracle at Alder Creek

58   Diastolic Metaphysics

59   Longer

61   I Can't Help Myself at the Buddhist Retreat

62   Aural Metaphysics

63   Languages I Don't Speak

65   The Piano Tuner Talks

66   Spring School

67   Night School

68   Death School

IV. Departure / Arrival

71   Advice to Himself Concerning the Voyage

72   Evening

73   Cuckoo: Tuscany

74   Economy Class

75   Owl

76   White Out

77   Scar

79   Six Encounters Before the Otter

80   Sloth

81   The End

82   The Sinister

83   Oxford

84   Gozo Poderoso

85   What the Wing Says

Wayne's College of Beauty

I know what wages beauty gives
                    —Yeats

We have dropped out of the other schools
to enroll here where no one fails; everything
is fixed, fluffed, teased into its temporary best
at cut-rate prices because we are all novices
in the art of making beauty, learning that beauty
is not so hard. Beauty is not so hard we learn,

because it is not chemicals or varieties of fashion.
Our scissors and combs, our libraries of lotions,
our bright mirrors assure the timorous or imperious
elderly they have come at last to the right place.
Wayne's is not the Heartbreak Hotel, and when they
leave beautiful, it is because they are briefly unlonely.

We have said, "How are you?" "How would you
like your hair?" and we have touched them not cruelly,
and with more than our hands. When it is over
we swivel their chairs so they can see themselves
carefully from several angles while we hover silent
just above their doubts, a calculation that provides
two faces in the mirror, ours smiling at both of us.

Fathers and Mothers

Husbands and Wives

Patriarch at the Lake

The aunts, splendid, pale
and ample in their bathing suits,
unfurl table cloths, challah, melons,
seltzer water in the blue bottles, and
honeyed cakes and other cakes.

After the required hour everyone
but Grandpa wades, stirring silt
around our ankles, squiggling mud,
enjoying the tickle of minnows

until, as if called by voices beyond
us, the old man rises, his belly taut,
trunks reaching his knees, his shins
white as fish, and walks without
watching the ground, toward water.

We part to let him pass, we recede
onto the beach; he prows outward
and swims. He remembers, he strokes
and roils and spumes his way away
then back to us, his shorebound spawn.

Practice: Father and Son

for Saul Swanger

The ball leaps toward my chest, misses
and takes a shot at my chin, leaving heat.

Dusk is a long inning, but darkness finally
rolls up, a low car with a quiet motor.

We can stop. I have fielded everything you hit,
but I ache with a kind of desire I will learn
is permanent and my gloved hand holds its sting.

Secrets

You should have been pacing all day, Father.
You should have been pondering your testicles.
You should have not let the slow sun latch
in place your dogged normalcy. What was
about to happen would not equate, Math Teacher,
and cannot now be engineered into benediction.

Someone you knew was on his way, dapper.
You liked his ease and pipe, and watched him
enter the unfledged ambition of my mother,
barely twenty, who pretended her own style,
liberated, *femme fatale*. I'm angry more than half
a century later. How pathetic we must have been,

my small hand in yours, while they left to test-
drive their liaison. You wished them a good week-
end. What were you thinking? And why tell me
this today, in a parking lot? We sit in the car
after her death, heat off the engine quietly ticking,
her afterlife, your years left, and mine, on an anvil.

I am so unforgiving, beating the living and dead
with my ancient hammer. Smashing old bones
into dust I choke on. I need to read some-
thing like *Gray's Anatomy*, and be touched by
the clinical comfort of death, how magnificent
are our mechanisms, our secrets revealed like jewels.

Assisted Living

I. Four Windows

More or less centered, geranium on the sill—
real, red, raggedy everyway absentmindedly.

The absence of decorations but this—a flag
decal dyed by sun; red to pink, blue to smoke.

Butterfly, angel, flower—translucent desire
arrayed, glommed on with spit and suction.

What could be an altar—the curtains cup
pumiceous light after a long day's journey.

II. View

Windows, windows on the wall,
Wanderings in the inner hall;
Porous bones buckle down
To work in the night's surround.

Passing windows and one another,
The elderly appear and remember
A hundred kisses, mild as milk,
Moving and still, synapses of silk.

III. Elevator

Bernie, rosy in his skin, proud in belly,
Noble in the weight of his genitals, enters
The elevator. No pants, no anything fully,
He gives me his back, to fasten suspenders.

Bernie flies memories like kites at the end
Of loose ends, and will do anything to please
Long dead Marsha, aflutter in the wind.
He takes her photo, murmurs, *"Say cheese."*

IV. Idea

There's a glint about old age that's sheer,
that's splinted by the past like shale
unfallen from the cliff wall, the sere
balance: weathered wood, hammered nail.

Standard time is not a given,
The hours ripen, tomatoes on stakes.
Each day its subdivision
Hands outstretched like upturned rakes.

We rummage hard-wrung remnants,
Shapes and shadows on the hard-baked plain.
Love, once thrown like books from a train,
Can be gathered up, read, and read again.

Debbie Does Daddy

Thinking of how fathers die, I want
insistence on order: that crackers
be lined up precisely by the soup

bowl, if there's soup; that no foot
jut from the bed's bone-colored
sheet in premature expectation of

a tag on the big toe; that breath, as
it clarifies finality, leave room for
a homespun confession, something

from father to son never said before.
Yet a friend declares with a smile,
"My father died a death we all want,"

after they found him rigid in the half-
light, witnessed only by a screen,
remote on hold, the single frame of

a porn film staring back. My friend
has the video now, *Debbie Does
Dallas*, and says he'd go the same

way, imagining himself fulfilled by
the mouth of a wanton girl. Not that I
believe tiers of angels will be laddered,

as in a Cimabue fresco, on each side
of my father's bed, not that his last
words will be deeply resonant—but

this is some angel to consider, the angel
of stained sheets and unembarrassed
openings, the angel who talks dirty and

bends over, the angel my friend's father
rented for the final, guttural afternoon.

Oedipus Irvington

Waverly 6-2829: sing this
to the tune of the Blue Danube
and you will know how
to call Grandma and Grandpa,
and you will never forget
the phone number of the cleanest
house in the world, in Irvington,
New Jersey, where you are left
to be admired and fed sweets
while your mother gives birth
to someone you will ignore as you
ignore your father except that he
brings you toys, or forgets the toy
he was supposed to bring; but Mom
loves you: you try to be bad as hard
as you have tried anything—harder—
still she thinks you are wonderful,
and this goes on for years, forever;
your life is a silver screen on which
you win Oscar after Oscar, but now
you want to retire from the movies
and it's as if you're the Mob;
there is no leaving with your shoes
on: you'll have to wear cement
galoshes to break this contract
that stipulates only success,
excellence, hazel-flecked eyes the girls
love of course—your mother's eyes.

My Mother's Nudes

Is it that I'm not done with you,
or that you are not done with me?
The person I love best says *stop*,
enough. But you tramp across
the page in the direction of your
failings, in the direction of your dreams.

We have unhappiness in common
as if in the blood. Nothing can be
enough. How many seductions would
it take? What could convince you, you
deserved to be loved? Those "art studies"
for which you posed naked: did they

love you, the men who made them?
Say yes, please. Say that you were loved
by some of them. Say that I will never
see the pictures. Let your ambition be
small and over. You're dead, and I've
had it. I want to be loved and left alone.

My Father: A Fiction

My father had a terrible childhood,
his own father selling apples on the street,
never completing his suicide in the closet,
then beginning to earn a dime here, and
there, in America, paving the backyard
and building a shop, hiring *schwartzes*.
My father would watch but not talk.

My father would not talk when his father
took him to the basement to welt his buttocks
with graceful flicks of whatever was handy.
Why did his father stop? After that, my father
at thirteen was nightly challenged by his father
to spar. To speed and feint of hand my father
lost every time before he could go to bed. He
watched this happen but would not say stop.

My father's mother watched but would not talk,
and after her husband's death, stayed where she
had always wanted to be, in one chair, with
a canary near by. Her legs grew elephantine and
she talked to the male bird, who was supposed
to sing despite the draped room, the never
come-and-go of anyone. What light there was, was
illegal, a trespasser. Her son felt himself a trespasser

entering the brocaded silence to ask if she needed
anything. When she needed to die, she couldn't.
She managed coma after coma, only coming close
to the death he wanted, her son. He secreted pills
over time, made a sweet paste of them and cream.
In the middle of his life, in the middle of her third
coma, as if she were an éclair waiting for a middle
of custard, he pumped the pills and cream into her.

He never told me about his terrible childhood, my father.
He never said his father could make a whip of anything
and had the reflexes of a welterweight. Or that his
parents lacked all affection. Or that in the end his
mother lived with a songless canary in a dark room.

Or that in the middle of trying to do what he planned carefully, he lost his nerve. And that in his life he was not evil, not decisive, not better, not loved enough.

The Past

Think of it as scrimshaw,
the tooth of a vulnerable giant,
adored and embellished by the same
hand which killed it—all that blood
sheening the surface as far as you can see.

Think of it as a sack of rags
ticking in the attic like a bomb,
a soft duffle in the corner, filled with
your cast-off skins unraveling imperceptibly
as they hold each other and whisper in the dark.

Think of it as your mother,
someone full of stories and baked goods
who tells you she forgives you no matter what,
while you forgive nothing you have done, and you
lash your tail like a cat trapped in her endless lap.

Think of it as irrevocably within
yourself, the meal you didn't taste
but know you have eaten, or the meal
that rises in your gorge the rest of your life,
when the table is empty, when all that remains are
the containers of several shapes; open, ingenious mouths.

The Old Are Different

The old are different, they level off
like Kansas when the rain's coming.
How suddenly desire vanishes, leaving
open space, phantom light—because
the storm's on its way. Now is the time
to call in the dogs. And if there are
horses, to shelter them from lightning.

The old are different, they do not sleep;
they smell ozone, they remember the ride
on the elevator, the following floors:
emergency, cardiac, cancer, stroke—and
what's the last one? They are unwilling
to give up their suffering, the albumen
in which they swim. And love, getting

bigger. The old become like ants who
carry several times their own weight.
Not spring, but they plant; not country,
but they remember constantly a prairie,
a dirt path, a child watching light change.
When they arrive, they enter calling to us
their idea of fun, "Hello! Hello! Anybody

home?" What good fortune to have them
among us. Everything makes them
conversational. They talk and it gets late,
and nothing is settled, and they are our
old, living like us with a fear. We go onto
the porch where we can see across the flat
land—we empty and refill the landscape.

The Lessons

The rules have changed—now
that so many fathers are dying
slow; the fathers of my generation
do not storm around on heaths
or rage as the light dims, or fall
to the sharper seasons of their sons.

Fathers diminish like fallen snow,
cease to shave daily, and emerge
from the bathroom unembarrassed
by the spots on their flies; they kiss
us at airports because something bad
will happen between now and then.

I refuse to inherit my father's house,
but return there for yet another lesson,
the lesson of the door laden with locks,
the lesson of the refrigerator's obdurate
optimism, the lesson of the interminable
insurance forms that attend his days,

the lesson of learning to lie down
domestic, apologies clouding the stars.

Alone

How to speak to our parents
and not make a mistake?

How to know that old age
is as lonely as childhood?

My childhood home is full
of my father who can't fill it.

No longer mowing the lawn,
taking down storm windows,

he drives at five in the morning,
every morning, to a gym

and rides a bicycle, watched
over by several TVs, into a land-

scape of Babel. With you gone,
I speak to my father who asks

how am I doing on my own.
I tell him I am untethered,

a balloon that can drift at any
moment, traceless, into space,

and that this is my loneliness.
I know, he says, I know.

My Daughter's Morning

My daughter's morning streams
over me like a gang of butterflies
as I, sour-mouthed and not ready
for the accidents I expect

of my day, greet her early:
her sparkle is as the edge of new
ice on leafed pools, while I
am soggy, tepid; old toast.

Yet I am the first version
of later princes; for all my blear
and bluish jowl I am welcomed
as though the plastic bottle

I hold were a torch and
my robe not balding terry.
For her I bring the day; warm
milk, new diaper, escapades;

she lowers all bridges and
sings to me most beautifully
in her own language while
I fumble with safety pins.

I am not made young
by my daughter's mornings;
I age relentlessly.

Yet I am made to marvel
at the durability of newness
and the beauty of my new one.

To Speak of the Woe

(cf. Robert Lowell)

"There was nothing I could do to save it,"
her husband tells her at dinner, the shiny
box empty of chicken nuggets. The slaw
grown warm, the Coke grown pale. Bad

news on the television. She dreamt last night
she was killed by carjackers. Shot twice,
she leaned back in the seat and gazed placidly
at nothing through the windshield. Or maybe

his face. He sees his reflection in the night
window. How high his forehead has become!
Does she desire him? "Don't feel guilty," she
says. "You'd've caused worse if you swerved.

Anyway what was it? A dog? Whatever—
it shouldn't have been there. You didn't wreck
the car. Stayed in your lane. You did okay."
Her husband wants her. Just one more demand.

The conversation annoys her. The future owns
them. Dents arrive daily, and they make one
payment after another. She'd give anything
for the silence of snakes mating, or dying.

Sleeping with You

for Lynn

The little bonus of
my hand on your hip.

Who needs the constellated sea?
All is as it should be.

Years on, you hold me still,
glamorous wind, pale star.

II.
Water
War

Natural Disaster

(Santa Cruz, California)

Overflow advances across strawberry
fields, insinuates streets and suddenly
everyone has a house on the water. And
such rich, redolent water, water carrying
land with it, effluents, aromas, stranded
cars, bodies in cars; water driving snakes
ahead of it, water augering through levees
and piling the fluid tonnage of itself against
bridges that break, great trees that swim
away from the bank and ride the roiling
surface until they are snagged by other
trees and slam sideways, trees logging up
into dams over which the river schusses.

The names of the creeks: Lompico, Bear,
Soquel, Zayante, Kings, Two Bar, Empire,
Aptos, Granite. And the rivers: Pajaro,
San Lorenzo. The names of the dead:
George, Leon, Sheila, Juan, Unknown and
Unknown. The names of the gods: Jaweh,
Father, Holy Spirit. The name of the lake
on whose bank grows a tree said to form
an image of the Virgin Mary in its bark:
Pinto. The name of the lucky one, not
home when his house slid over the edge:
Robert. The name of the thing that brings
the rivers up and the hills down: rain.

Flood

Tie down the pianos! The waltzes are
sodden, the tourist barges besieged
by mud. The mouths of the palaces
drown in the Elbe, the Danube, rivers
that have no respect for history, for
great bridges across which conquering

Christians clattered, lances piercing
the sky now filled with rain upon rain.
The stones of Prague, Dresden, Plzeň
go soft, begin to resemble Venice.
As once Noah saved the animals, zoo
officials rescue giraffes, elephants,

penguins, storks, gorillas. A blind-
folded rhino dangles in a red sling from
a helicopter. One doesn't want to fly
and meets its end. Grim tonnage, as
grim as the future of history. Our
effluvia have warmed the sky, brought

the tropics to Europe, water to the base-
ment of the Zwinger Palace, the Semper
Opera, the Mala Strana. How happy
the five seals, escaped from their concrete
confinement into the rushing Vltava,
the new emperors of the baroque city.

Spoken Wading In

yes I wrote "Observe Everything"
in my diary and yes I put haddock
on the stove and yes I likened my
life to a great wave and yes the great
wave accumulated its mass through
minutiae and yes I walked into water
holding a stone to my belly like
a child and yes I applied hydraulic
pressure to every word and yes
the things around my ankles did
frighten me and yes because I could
still feel something I almost stopped
and yes I aspired to the impossible
as the still life aspires to be truly
still and yes the greatest problem
is knowing and yes I've found a
solution and yes there is no insistent
clarity and yes a restful gauzing over

What Burns on Water

All along the Ganges the black smell,
the Ghats where bodies are brought, one
after the other, burned on the altars on
the water, smoke so continuous it is no
more noticed than the small lapping, the
river's monologue as it notices here an
arm, unburnt, or there a foot, unburnt,
fallen from the Ghat like errant kindling,
the yellow water in which children play,
elders think to purify themselves, ritually
immersing themselves five times a day,
mouths thirsty for holiness, the water held
sacred even as it dies. And the burning

of a great ship leaning into the languid
Atlantic, boilers ablaze, prow dividing and
dividing all that's ahead, another continuous
burning, day and night while passengers
dress for dinner, undress for sleep or love,
tango in the low-ceilinged salon, above fires
driving the hull, the steady underwater roar,
the mythology of monsters. And when the
vessel noses blunt against a city's silhouette,
a ringing of fireboats shoots plumes shining
as if the ocean had been conquered by this
burning, the trail left below and above, the
smudged sky joining water. And the burning

of tragedy fallen from the sky in an early
instance, Icarus, so full of the sun it became
a sudden weight, a hammer beating him
into the sea where he left a glimmer; where
Cleopatra's boats, oars like broken wings,
burned; where Moses bent the sea back upon
itself to save some and kill others, and Christ,
with dexterity, magic or both, walked above a
cloud of fishes before he died. Destinations of
the greatest burning take us across the water;

behind us the bridges clang and we are borne
suddenly at an odd angle, at cross-purposes
and toward a passing, through

Seasons / Water

*

A dead cormorant
floats in place.
What a nuisance, autumn.

*

Winter rain
writing on earth.
A good time for surgery.

*

Amber kelp below;
and look it's flowered!
Why so sad, sea turtle?

*

A ten foot swell pushes
the kayak sideways.
Like Ishmael, I meet my coffin.

Jews, Those

Who place pebbles   Who place pebbles   Who place pebbles   Who place pebbles   Who place pebbles
On headstones   On headstones   On headstones   On headstones   On headstones
Of the graves   Of the graves   Of the graves   Of the graves   Of the graves
Of their people   Of their people   Of their people   Of their people   Of their people
Before they go   Before they go   Before they go   Before they go   Before they go

Who place pebbles   Who place pebbles   Who place pebbles   Who place pebbles   Who place pebbles
On headstones   On headstones   On headstones   On headstones   On headstones
Of the graves   Of the graves   Of the graves   Of the graves   Of the graves
Of their people   Of their people   Of their people   Of their people   Of their people
Before they go   Before they go   Before they go   Before they go   Before they go

Who place pebbles   Who place pebbles   Who place pebbles   Who place pebbles   Who place pebbles
On headstones   On headstones   On headstones   On headstones   On headstones
Of the graves   Of the graves   Of the graves   Of the graves   Of the graves
Of their people   Of their people   Of their people   Of their people   Of their people
Before they go   Before they go   Before they go   Before they go   Before they go

Who place pebbles   Who place pebbles   Who place pebbles   Who place pebbles   Who place pebbles
On headstones   On headstones   On headstones   On headstones   On headstones
Of the graves   Of the graves   Of the graves   Of the graves   Of the graves
Of their people   Of their people   Of their people   Of their people   Of their people
Before they go   Before they go   Before they go   Before they go   Before they go

Who place pebbles   Who place pebbles   Who place pebbles   Who place pebbles   Who place pebbles
On headstones   On headstones   On headstones   On headstones   On headstones
Of the graves   Of the graves   Of the graves   Of the graves   Of the graves
Of their people   Of their people   Of their people   Of their people   Of their people
Before they go   Before they go   Before they go   Before they go   Before they go

Who place pebbles   Who place pebbles   Who place pebbles   Who place pebbles   Who place pebbles
On headstones   On headstones   On headstones   On headstones   On headstones
Of the graves   Of the graves   Of the graves   Of the graves   Of the graves
Of their people   Of their people   Of their people   Of their people   Of their people
Before they go   Before they go   Before they go   Before they go   Before they go

Who place pebbles   Who place pebbles   Who place pebbles   Who place pebbles
On headstones   On headstones   On headstones   On headstones
Of the graves   Of the graves   Of the graves   Of the graves
Of their people   Of their people   Of their people   Of their people
Before they go   Before they go   Before they go   Before they go

The Coming War

Someone takes a '39 Dodge,
delicately lifts the body laced
with rust off the frame, hopes
the frame will hold, and begins.

A shaft of titanium is installed
where my femur was, and meets
the acetabulum that provides
a pivot: metal now better than bone.

Today the dentist inserts a needle
five times to numb the fractured
and still cracking tooth. Nice not
to feel the drill, the hollowing out.

There are so many ways we can hold
together against time. Truly, we live
longer and longer, as do our cars. So
why does the dog growl at something

he hears on the other side of the door?
Each time I go to look the air is empty.
Still, I take the dog's word for it:
there is no lack of menace on earth.

Oh Dear Ones: 9/11/01

Let's talk about the edge of the world

where nothing is supposed to happen
except Keats, the self-possession of beauty.
The earth rolls away, polishing itself
as it goes. Could this be? Where are we after
scenarios that end us? My wife has a circular
view: things are as they were before we were.
The after is the before. And so, can I bury into
the future this word, or day, the terrible one?

It's a long view. Hard to keep bright. Pass
the salt, I'd like to say, knowing there are miles
of bad luck between us and the sea. So sky
passes us, our burned-out white dust, wind over
wind, toward water. And all that scuffling,
the shouts, the astonishing flash of pain, become
distance riding above the survivors. Oh dear
ones that died, oh dear ones that search the dust.

State of the Union: February 2003

All this hugging: on the street, in hallways, in restaurants, in queues. In public. Public hugging. (No hugs on Grecian urns, says Keats) Are we a warm nation? Bear hugs. Thug hugs. Designer hugs. The hugs of relatives. Hollywood hugs. Presidential hugs. Lesser political hugs. Socialite hugs. Jock hugs. Gay hugs.

"What we do battle with is so small," Rilke wrote, "What battles us is so large."

Taking A Bite

The day has hardly begun, shark gray,
and the sky takes a bite out of the day.

Like the big bite we call love, tenderly
administered, changing everything, or

gone, leaving everything scarred. No
one uses that word anymore, "hickey,"

for little love bites, a girl in a tank top
expertly nipping her boyfriend's neck.

Too old, too sure that sex has meaning,
our hope is erotic and an intimation

of failure. We take shape as a flight
over the ocean. From this altitude we

see several shark-dark shadows just
beneath the surface; the shoreline darts

in and out. Small cavorting figures,
as predictable as love, enter the water.

Regime Change

On the beach thirteen new-cut poles;
bound to each by wire, a cabinet minister.

The men stare ahead, or perhaps back at what
has brought them to this. The nearly naked
ministers hear their history wafting out to sea,
sinking among the sway of those already dead.

The line between sea and sand is not a line.
The ministers enter silence while their
old titles beat hard between their ribs.
The executioner mumbles official charges,

his pistol heavy, his forearm weary. Him.
One gun. Thirteen ministers. How many did
thirteen ministers kill, each a conductor raising
his baton, his cocked wrist aiming his hand here

and there?   Night begins the unsleep of widows
who lift their skirts just above sand and bodies,
precise in this wading, circumspect as herons
highstepping, disliking the water they depend on.

The women are brides manacled to ash
and lamentation, to odors that cannot be erased,
to sitting by the road, to the unforgiving moon,
to uniforms scaly with medals, the new regime.

The Uses of Sky

Let the weather be bad—no sun brewing
primordial soup, new life that might prove
god. Pewter sky shows to good advantage
the red-dolloped koi, and the one wide-bodied
and gold-leafed, and another of too many colors

and flashes to name. Stones at the bottom
clamor like sex. Look how voluptuous I am
the breast-shaped little boulders cry out. They
are drowned but don't know it. The fish can
only circle but don't know what a circle is.

Such innocence! The unspeakable things we do
are better done in the sun. Not the dark where they
are expected, but in so much light the edge of their
infamy fades. Men have been hanged from yardarms,
sent to fishes, sunk like rocks, in the dazzle of noon.

Whoever's Nearest

Here we are in the roar again, the subway,
in the forest of souls that bend with no mind
of their own. Start: sway toward the back.
Stop: sway toward the front. The air is close;
the light, unnatural; the door locked between
illusions of free will. No one's going anywhere;
it's time for one person to get to know another.
Whoever's nearest. "What of the war?" I say
to the older woman staring ahead, at nothing.
"Has it started?" The woman knows exactly
how gray the world is above, and about
the unspeakable clarity of flames sinuous in
the streets, dropped as we speak, from the sky.

III.
Known
Unknown

Wayne's College of Beauty

Asteroids Advance Toward Earth

The woman across the way comes out
each night resplendent and distended.
She lowers herself onto the low curb,
her dark legs splayed, the baby inside

her within the large ball she holds on her
lap. Vivid and factual, she tells us about
someone with lupus maybe dying, maybe
just sick forever. He's young, and his wife

who's older has nerves that ring constantly.
Other neighbors arrive, following their dogs'
noses as their dogs reckon odiferous ghosts,
and slowly lift their legs to bless the roses.

What does it mean, the objects of our affection
unleashed and leading us into the gentle night,
while someone about to burst tells us that,
amid the asteroids, we are lucky to be here?

Style

For Elissa

There are so many rules
it takes good luck to live
long enough to break them.

I guess profoundly to undo
the manifesto requires
more than longevity: style

is the ultimate morality
of the mind, says Whitehead,
as if the mind were a rector

standing stylishly at the door,
or elegant on the chair's edge
overhearing this conversation

between you and me. I hope
you will not listen to teachers
who say never paint in black.

Paint in black, bathe in black,
wear black at your wedding,
something so moral it resonates

you into Gothic thunder and
everyone blinks, and cannot
believe anything they knew

before. Send them into the cave
of their hearts, my heart, send
them into the deep, deep dark.

Aubade

It's early and the dark says, "We are pleased to inform you,"
and on the ground stands a great horned owl making eye

contact as if you are equals; and when the light comes it
assumes the shape of trees, and dawn begins to saturate

a snakeskin in the grass. Something shudders the bushes.
Where will you go? Hold out your hands, gather in the

noise of birds; this space is wider than you can ever fill.
Could life be better? Or more? Tell me, how many hawks?

Uncertainty Principle

The dog tosses a handful
of seagulls into the air.
Where will they land?

Miracle at Alder Creek

Frost-bitten, stranded in canyon,
woman says angels kept her alive.
                    —The Oregonian

We are one geography, and hunger for
how she survived, the elk hunter who
fell, injured, in a pine-covered forest
and lay there seven nights. It's not
enough she already had diabetes and
asthma; moonbright in Alder Creek

Canyon, at four below zero, the cold
"would just suck through you, pull
every bit of strength out of you," Ken
Nash, a Mormon bishop in Enterprise,
Oregon, said. And the same elk she
was hunting broke the 6-inch ice of

Alder Creek so she could palm water
into her mouth. "The best way to
describe it was two lights in the shape
of two people," she said. They appeared
after she began to pray, rendered against
the snow; and they said nothing, vanished

at daybreak, but stayed with her through
each night. "We witnessed a true miracle,"
according to Wallowa Sheriff Fred Steen.
And everything I'm telling was in the paper
except that she foraged on her knees among
goldfinches for berries, rose hips and moss.

Diastolic Metaphysics

The Romantic in the heart cries its
heart out over a sparrow, yet believes

in immortality. The Rational in the heart
searches the garden for a downpour

to glaze the wheelbarrow, to polish
the tensile fretwork of a dragonfly.

The heart would know itself, no matter
the suspect gods, ravening appetites,

sad clocks, the horizon deckled
into a succession of small stabs felt

like the anxiety of faith. The little red
sack knows it fills and empties, and

wonders where it was written that
it must remain unfinished and suffer.

Longer

for Lauren

It is the beginning of that long,
soft silence when the household
sleeps. My daughter should be
in her bed, but instead she asks
me why she must die, and what
there is after death. The girl
glistens, a rosy dolphin riding
swells of seamless health and youth,
yet she worries. She stays awake
into the night like an astronomer
captive to his cold telescope.
If sleep has its opposite, it is
not waking, but the imagination.

I can't answer questions like hers,
but I can make up the necessary
stories. Two hundred years ago in Italy,
the voices of boys were so pure
the music maestros of the cities
preserved the dazzle of this sound
by creating choirs of castrati, and
penned operas for the smooth-jawed
sopranos these boys grew up to be.
In wide-windowed Venice there
seemed no end to the glorious singing,
as if birds from heaven had chosen
to alight and stay forever joyful
in the porticos and gilded arches.

My daughter thinks this has nothing
to do with death although it is
very cruel, the razor the old guys
inflicted upon those boys, the abortion
of nature in the lives of so many
who had been innocently harvesting
olives, singing for no particular
reason, for no imaginable audience,
certainly not for the desiccated

aesthetes overdressed in brocade
and velvet who changed everything
so swiftly and irrevocably. Don't
get me wrong, I tell my daughter,
I'm not for gelding singers to save
their voices: the idea is to sing,
very beautifully, a little longer.

I Can't Help Myself at the Buddhist Retreat

for Max

I confess to having doubts about Eastern spirituality.
Else why set off my car alarm at the monastery?
An accident? Calm and folded, the monks sit *zazen*,
going into the great space inside themselves, all of them.
I have just arrived in the elaborate quiet, the canyon of less,
hot enough that blue-bellied lizards abandon their push ups
and appear to meditate; even the ceaseless jays have ceased.
My feet detonate puffs of dust as I abstractly saunter away
from the car in an attempt to deny the wailing is mine. I've
forgotten how to shut down this unseemly fervor, this insistent
ululation, a word I've wanted to use for a long time. But not here.

Aural Metaphysics

The sound of one hand clapping
is the sound of the other shoe dropping;
is the bird in the bush wondering where
is the sad bird, the one in the hand; is
the sound of a newspaper delivering bad
news; is the mother tongue of someone
whose mother told her to hold her tongue;
is the sound of the wishbone that arcs
in yearning, that you left to dry on the sill.

Languages I Don't Speak

for Lynn

I.

There are many languages I don't speak,
including the essential one, sleep, which
could be the language that enables all
the others. Or maybe being up at four, my
tongue coated with Scotch, is my language.

Nothing makes a difference in this vocabulary
because everything is so important: how
I love you, how I can't say a word to you now
because you need your sleep. It's all miles

beyond simile. There's no moon rising like
thought, no wing—at last—lifting me in its
illusory style above the mother you would
not have in this poem, or any other: "Dammit,

get your mother out of the poem; you are
married to me!"   And yes it's true. And I
would gladly jump in front of the bullet so you
might live and walk out of the alley intact,

the inconsequential alley where I expect to die
over a foolish dispute—no, over something even
more foolish, an expectation that years of push-
ups and bench presses prepare me for anything.

II.

I am prepared for nothing: the mugger, the long
chase down the alley during which my surgically
repaired leg reveals that stitching is not wholeness.
Wasn't the Leonardo cartoon of the Virgin Among

The Rocks slashed by one twentieth century man,
repaired by another?— and remains slashed,
although a rare testament to the healing art of art,
curators able to expound on what has happened,

reversing history, if you will, not to a canvas un-
slashed, but seeming unslashed even as the meticulous
record of the knife's work, the technicians' miracle to
undo the knife's work, leaves us the illusory whole.

III.

Nothing is more fragile than the laughter we take
for granted, that we can gather around our lives
and laugh at what continues to happen to us,

as Leonardo would laugh at the sad and active soul
who didn't merely stand housebroken before the cartoon
of the Virgin and her elderly, meaty-armed Christ child.
He took a knife to the canvas, and—I'm not sure of this
as a metaphor—it's time to take knife to canvas, unskillfully

to the canvas where life can be revealed. I tried, and found
the gravestones of the Jewish cemetery in Prague where
the dead are layered twelve deep. So much of me there, I
wish I were there, wholly unheroic, listing toward another

stone while you, in accordance to custom, pick up a
pebble from the tribe of everlasting peoples, and place it,
as the best memorial we have devised so far, upon
a bright rising of dark words, hard pebble on a hard crypt.

The Piano Tuner Talks

Birds don't tune up, far as I know, tracing their
tremulos on high wires. Nor do whales, billowers
of melodramatic ballads. So much depends,
as they say, on these notes; and so little goes into

them of practice or anxiety. We know the piano is
fraught: consider 230 strings, each tortured to 170
pounds of tension, 20 tons of torsional pull in all:
the unbearable heaviness of the mazurka, the étude,

the Joplin rag once *de rigeur* at weddings. I'm
hearing less lately and could quit. An electronic
device would listen for me if I let it. Still, I know
the piano is a voice waiting to sing, requires me to still

what should not move—string, soundboard, bridge
and pins—requires me to calibrate humidity—and I must,
trust me, hit every key brutally, severally, to ensure
it plays true, that what I've put there, stays there.

Spring School

Early enrollment encouraged; such
a twitter in the auditorium, light
about to enter. The lecture of cherry
blossoms: absence, absence, absence,
and then brevity, beauty to which we
can anchor nothing. In the academy
of fragile questions, we spend it all
on tuition. Think small, the lessons
say, think now. Let us learn to weave
twigs. Leaves begin their edges;
the air is full of syllables. Our inner
arm maps a country of veins. Let us
write about the risks taken by flowers.

Night School

The dark, the stars,
the light, the way
the vendor stirs
her flat black pan,
the inconsolable
candle, the story
asleep on a pillow
of invented terrors,
the long hallway to
the welder's where
flowers of sparks
bloom and burn.

Death School

Everybody graduates. We become
darkness, we are diplomas unfurled
in a language older than Latin, we
march down the aisle of kerchiefs;
we leave footprints that fill with water.

We are about to begin our life's work.
Congratulations! We will sow handfuls
of names; we will make the snow human;
we will fool around with night, and
cause stars to disappear, to shine, to fall.

IV.
Departure
Arrival

Advice to Himself Concerning the Voyage

Don't worry yet about lust, about
being lashed to the mast and hearing
voices. Think Platonically: build
the boat as if it will carry ideas.

Or focus on a different father.
Noah in his elephantine ark, given
another chance. Why Noah? Why
you? You've never won anything; so

don't get carried away by size. Maybe
a dory will do, and you will feel a thirst
when it arrives, a craving for slow rivers
that enter the sea, the face of the sea,

candid and treacherous. This is an old
image and no reason to think you'll
succeed by wind or by oar. The sailor
you resemble most is Popeye. So eat

your spinach; forget about the half-built
boat in the basement, its splinted ribs crying
out, its smell of tar and future of leaks.
Climb the stairs; Olive Oyl waits.

Evening

I.

Cloud that never moved,
frog-faced cloud,
is gone.

II.

Between boat and shore
a long step.
Don't fall in!

III.

Beneath the eaves sparrows
tuck heads under wings.
Cat looks for cat.

Cuckoo: Tuscany

He thought there were no birds to sing,
all of them for centuries snared by wire
fine as grass: lark, finch, thrush, fox
sparrow, pipit, dove, even the wren
become fractions of meals, birds barely
a mouthful, pliable bones, specks of flesh.

Yet the brown cuckoo in Tuscany insists
it is alive. Not a pleasant bird, but alive:
cuckoo—cuckoo—cuckoo—cuckoo
intersects with silence, owns acres of
air, wedges its repetition between hills.
No stopping this two-syllable cousin

of Poe's raven, this parasite among birds
with a history of eggs in nests not its own
from which fledgling cuckoos dispatch
the rightful heirs to their death. A bird
whose beak curves like a scythe, whose
call could be fuck you, fuck you, fuck you.

A bird right for the region whose families,
Baglioni, degli Oddi, Ranieri, the Arcipreti,
murdered, by defenestration, each other
in accord with ancient contract. The light here
does not reveal its source. Illumination is
everywhere. And the sound of the cuckoo,

the recognition of abiding. Under what
pretext could beauty shine less, be lesser?
Coming to these hills from elsewhere, he
believes himself virtuous, unmarred as if
desire enacts no cost. The bird that's left
bears witness, a braggart sound at a distance.

Economy Class

He bulges down the aisle, necessarily sideways,
eyes the drink cart and its multitude of miniatures.
His is the complexion of a monkey's prick.
He sidles closer and closer, larger and larger, effluvial.

During frequent indolence, baboons casually
fuck. The male opens her flower-swollen
and besmirched petals by inserting his pencil
of a prick. She reaches back to give it one touch
with one finger before resuming nonchalance.

He levers himself into the proximal seat,
takes possession of the arm rest, extends
his pinky ring. "I'm Don." "Hi Don!" (You
old monkey prick!) Don begins twinking
his teeth and his fingers; Don hopes the stewardess
and her hips will swivel this way. In the meantime
it's too tight to fidget. Don fidgets. Where is she?
We're closer than apes in the closest cage in the zoo.

Owl

The owl, the most silent flyer,
flies on the softest feathers,
sees by the smallest moonlight
the vole, the mice among grasses,

and the rabbit. In the owl quiet,
in the owl shadow, those who are
left await their turn. The owl is
someone in a white coat in a room.

White Out

He doesn't mind that his hair is a beach
losing its battle with the tide; or
that the vertebrae of his lower back grind
toward shriek like frayed wires between
poles waiting for the indifferent wind.

He wonders how he knew so little, he
buying one car after another, good deals;
he getting degrees and jobs, an office
with a view of people coming to ask his
permission, his wife tentative and tender.

There was so much to control, he kept
a calendar, compiled a resumé, built
a house around the dimensions of his knees,
the stack of his wife's crockery, the years
his children would require those bathrooms.

He didn't wonder and he didn't wait, and
when his daughter scratched the latest car
he was proud to be moderately mad. Before
his wife went shopping she asked him what
he'd like to eat that week, not much meat.

Half his life was things to do, and done,
checked off; he looks now at the grid of days,
the pages of months, and writes in nothing
although nothing has changed; he buys bottles
of White-Out in case he makes a mistake, but

with so much arranged there is no need.
He hears a siren, not the police kind.
A whispered insistent question that has
nothing to do with peaches comes to him
in the wide space of night. He watches

the trajectories of planes so distant
they make no sound, so sure amid the web
of radar it would appear there are no
people in the sky, only the blind lights,
each blinking at the tip of its wing.

Scar

The truth is never enough
but I'll tell it anyway:
this scar was once a blue
bird with a forked tail,
applied by the staccato
prick of the tattooist's
electric needle behind
the dusty glass off Broad
Street in Newark, N.J.,
on a day when peace marchers
and pickpockets shuffled
toward police barriers.

This blue bird with its
forked tail was the reason
you left me and my left biceps,
my upper arm flexor, which
made the bird fly or hover
and stoop from the flesh-
colored sky my arms supported
above your body before
you enrolled in Language
Studies at Princeton where
your maiden name could speak
after its prolonged silence.

This reason was the abrasive
wheel in the doctor's office
(having found an ad, "Tattoos
Removed," in the Yellow Pages),
among the aquariums full of dying
fish where my skin was flayed
flying off me like soft sparks,

blood, ink, and flesh into the air.
I left with a clumsy bandage and
the old man's promise there
would be no scar, no evidence
of all these fallen feathers.

The scar is because I'm black
the doctor said to my white
face while his fish watched.
"Black people form more keloid
tissue; it's not my fault," OK,
being black is no problem, but
this is a big scar something
like the blue bird with a forked
tail, and my biceps makes the scar
fly toward an apparition
of a pale bird just visible
inside the shape of itself.

Which is why I probably am
too hard on both of us,
creating these collisions now,
like the bird who comes down
the chimney into our lives
and bangs its life out against
the window even though we try
to save it, and tells us
something as we pick up
the weightless body, the irrational
broken neck and the single bead
of blood losing its luster.

Six Encounters Before the Otter

First there is *water*, which holds nothing in its hands
(well, maybe a sheen of salt or palette of oil). And
collects *light* like a movie screen where wonders will
happen. Some dog may part the water into a *kiss* that
loves the dog and keeps its intentions from the mouth

below. Through it all, the *sun* tells time like a flower
most open at noon (think of Linnaeus' clock of flowers,
tolling hours by each species' bloom). Then there is
wisdom at the end of the muddy estuary where an otter,
at first surprised by us, dives, then reappears because

the *mind*, whatever it is, cannot get enough of the world.

Sloth

I am the microphone after the sweat,
I am the stain of power misspent,
the silent coves where promises thicken
to sludge; I am inexorable torpor,
the spirit overwhelmed and shrunk.

Imagine the most complex problem
of all, let's say a rain forest, or food,
or the true believers of a bad book.

Here are the answers: drive any-
where and feel free; eat ice, what's
frozen can't hurt you; go to school.

I could say more, but I don't want to.
I am the prophet of less: a single feather
bespeaks the bird and a sigh suffices
for love. It's come to this: believe me,
you don't have to run to find cover.

The End

(after Montale)
for Ivan Rosenblum

How the *galop* halts, the notes caught
in your hair, the tempo, the light in your eyes,
the anxiety of one note, of many, of a chord,
and the tremor of sadness in your wrists,
your silent mouth. How you are, sitting
at the piano, ready to leave me.

The Sinister

Once we expected the sinister
to look sinister, deformed: maybe
a hump or a hook or a club foot.
Or the sinister place, slimed and
ill lit. Chains dangling, bones
in the broken ballet of bones. Or
nature, sinister in tooth and claw:
sharks, snakes, mobs of wolves
after us, always almost winning.

The sinister is worse than folk tales.
The sinister looks like the kid next
door who wears glasses, the sinister
sounds like a small lie, a heart bereft
and waiting, a book. The sinister is
a book, sinister sewn into its lining,
releasing sincere, ineradicable words.
Sinister is a mirror beaming back.

After the sinister happens, we knew
it was coming. There was something
odd about that kid. And the man who
was dumped, by his wife, by his boss,
evicted from the barrack of his brain—
we knew his heart was a land mine.
We knew that the farmer who painted
"Cow!" on the side of his cows would
find the cows shot anyway the next day.

Oxford

We come through the scalloped stone
steps worn away by so many heavy
with learning and piety, and out
into the motors and metal air that
surround the Bodleian like a soiled
curtain; and we drift toward the only
green, the old common where long-
horned, curly cattle hold their hugeness
as if it were ordinary to graze here
for a thousand years, since wolves.

There is a thickly thatched stone barn,
the roof at once sliding down and solid;
and the farmer, red, robust, a Mellors
with his braces on, takes us into the kind
of confidence we offer strangers who are
truly strange and soon to depart. His magic
is such that bulls low to him when he calls.
He tells us of barn owls under the thatch,
and we climb into the dark to see them.
The moons of their faces watch us ascend.

The male owl unscrolls one wing, written
upon delicately, and with this wing he
shields his mate from us. Their clutch
of owlets hisses at us, a sound wind draws
from sharp grasses. The owlets condemn us.
Righteous and robed, they are a committee,
and we descend the ladder afraid. Since
it's Oxford, I think of Thomas More at study,
climbing a ladder to the highest of shelves,
and what he saw there before he turned.

Gozo Poderoso

God, it is reported, when he made the world,
made it so big he had to make himself smaller.
"Oy, there's no room in the world for me
as I am," God may have said; or he may
have said, "Where is there room for the world,
I'm so big? Oy!" And with that or without
that, God moved himself into servant's quarters.

He works hard, there are so many concerns. He
works hard, there are so many cracks in our
character, in containers—he sweats like a welder.
The domed helmet, eyes invisible behind glass.
Blacked out, he traffics in sparks so you and I
can hog the couch and consider radically different
conclusions while resting on our elbows. We

easily push open a door to get a banana, a book,
to know the world is real. Our books are full of
famous people and contradictions. We invent
attitude, metaphor, an untutored attachment to
sunlight, language like "gozo poderoso" which
means *powerful joy*, if we want it to. The word
while it can, plays energetically at theatres everywhere.

What the Wing Says

The wing says, "I am the space behind you,
a dent in the fender, hands you remember
for the way they touched you. You can look
back and song will still throb. I am air
moving ahead, the outermost edge of desire,
the ripple of departure and arrival. But

I will speak more plainly: you think you are
the middle of your life, your own fulcrum,
your years poised like reckonings in the balance.
This is not so: dismiss the grocer of your soul.
Nothing important can be weighed, which is why
I am the silver river of your mornings and
the silver lake curled around your dark dreams.
I am not wax nor tricks stolen from birds.

I know you despair at noon, when the sky overflows
with the present tense, and at night as you lie
among those you have wronged; I know you have failed
in what matters most, and use your groin to forget.
Does the future move in only one direction?
Think how roots find their way, how hair spreads
on the pillow, how watercolors give birth to light.
Think how dangerous I am, because of what I offer you."

David Swanger lives in Santa Cruz, California, with his wife, Lynn. His awards include an NEA fellowship in poetry and the Foley Award from America magazine. He is the author of four previous book-length poetry collections, two chapbooks, and two nonfiction books. He holds degrees from Swarthmore College and Harvard University.